D1428794

WATER SESSIONS

WATER SESSIONS

James Lasdun

CAPE POETRY

Published by Jonathan Cape 2012

2 4 6 8 10 9 7 5 3 1

Copyright © James Lasdun 2012

James Lasdun has asserted his right under the Copyright, Designs
and Patents Act 1988 to be identified as the author of this work

First published in Great Britain in 2012 by
Jonathan Cape
Random House, 20 Vauxhall Bridge Road,
London SW1V 2SA

www.randomhouse.co.uk

Addresses for companies within The Random House Group Limited can be found at:
www.randomhouse.co.uk/offices.htm

The Random House Group Limited Reg. No. 954009

A CIP catalogue record for this book
is available from the British Library

ISBN 9780224097093

The Random House Group Limited supports The Forest Stewardship Council
(FSC®), the leading international forest certification organisation. Our books
carrying the FSC label are printed on FSC® certified paper. FSC is the only
forest certification scheme endorsed by the leading environmental organisations,
including Greenpeace. Our paper procurement policy can be found at:
www.randomhouse.co.uk/environment

Typeset by Palimpsest Book Production Limited,
Falkirk, Stirlingshire
Printed and bound in Great Britain by
the MPG Books Group, Bodmin, Cornwall

in memory of my father

CONTENTS

WATER SESSIONS

THE SKATERS

Their town's the quaint one:
the board won't let it sprawl
more than a half mile from the green's
little pool-table of grass and shiny tulips
where Santa lands in winter and the teens
play hackysack all summer. There's no mall,

no motel either,
which is just what they want;
they voted for the good life there;
they can afford it: no fastfood chain, no sixplex,
they'll quietly brag; no trailer park, no air-
or groundwater-fouling autoshop or plant . . .

You'll find all that here
in the next town along.
You'll know you've reached us when you pass
a smooth vast meadow with a thousand white pipes
curved down like candycane, venting the gas
from their buried garbage. Then all the usual wrong

do-able by men
to a stubborn landscape,
to settle it and make it pay,
goes reeling by; the usual aching and craving
risen on blasted granite and raw clay.
They point their finger and they call it rape,

and maybe they're right,
though from some viewpoints, folks
might think them hypocritical,
like how they bring their kids to the new Kiwanis
ice-rink – the kids all slim and tall
from too little junk-food (one of our little jokes) –

every damn weekend.
Not that they're not welcome –
anyone can come here that wants:
here's failure without the allure, here's the mirage
gone from marriage; beer guts slung over pants,
butts like boulders in spandex, hard mouths home

on weekend parole;
here the abused and creased,
the maimed-in-spirit, the tainted
(what by, no-one remembers or cares any more)
totter out on their blades to get reacquainted
with sheer effortless rapture, or at least

the idea of it:
that frictionless surface
gets scratched and bleared up before long,
then turns to a thick, grey, gravelly slurry
which, we have to admit, is easier-going,
maybe because it reminds us of us,

though for a moment,
the page of ice still bare,
we're just like them again: all flow,
our stumblings still not written, the world so primed
we're back believing where we want to go
we'll get to, just by *wishing* ourselves there.

INSTEAD

Having already thwarted
your wish to explain,
your need to call to account,
by being his own judge, jury
and executioner,
the man with the heavy backpack
boards the crowded train

where a half awake
assortment of private lives
jostling towards completion
on their own terms, at their own pace,
are about to become the point he was trying to make
when he lost his thread,
putting it this way instead.

THE BLIGHT

What's there to say? We didn't care for him much,
and you can't exactly commiserate
with someone you don't just not love
but almost (admit it) hate.
So the news just hung over us
like the dud summer weather we'd had –
rain since June, the lawn sodden,
garden a bog, all slugs, late blight so bad
our sickened Beefsteak vines, our Sweet One Hundreds,
San Marzanos, the lot,
yellowed half black before the fruit had set,
which, when it did, began to bloat and rot
before it ripened – but like I say
(and not to speak ill of the dead)
we just didn't care for him,
which is probably all there is to be said.

THE QUESTION

We're eating outside with our friends,
Woodstock Buddhists; our kids and theirs
are lighting sticks on citronella candles
to throw them at the woods like burning spears;
the Rainbow Family of Living Light
are drumming in Magic Meadow; I've drunk enough
that all I want to do is close my eyes,
when a voice rings like a summons from the darkness:
my six-year-old son asking: 'Dad,
is America good or bad?'

He's heard us talking; the litany:
stolen elections, torture memos, wars;
seen the picture of the hooded man –
Haj Ali, our oppressor-victim,
arms spread, posed on his box
like Jesus on his mountain
blessing the peacemakers
(but for the dangling wires)
and wants to know whose side he's on:
his own or someone else's side against him . . .

What can I say? *That depends*
on what you mean by 'good' or 'bad'
or for that matter 'America',
which might be a fool and his goons
war-gaming in the White House,
but might be, say, the Women in Black
down on the Green with their banner, 'Bring Our Troops Back',
or the Rainbow People up in the meadow
drumming in the full moons,
or might just be us and our friends . . . ?

He's waiting for his answer.
I open my mouth to speak
but something stalls me; a strange
heaviness on my tongue
as if after all I'd pledged silence
or struck some nocturnal pact
over whatever act,
doubtful or downright wrong,
secures our presence here,
and I can't seem to say a damn thing,

and he drifts away, back to his game
of fending off the trees
that look as though they'd marched up the hill
to mass at the edge of our lawn
while we sat here talking,
and a dim shame
clouds in as if there were really something to do
other than drink and chill
and listen to the drums beat
and try to keep our eyes open.

STORM

Driving towards them at dusk
I thought they were tree-stumps:
first-growth hemlocks, storm-felled
decades ago, their trunks carted off for lumber,

but I had my dimensions wrong:
what the twilight had rounded out
and turned to rotting wood, was flat
mossed-over stone. They were gravestones,

tilted that way by frost. I drove on,
out of the wind and lightning
my mind had conjured in error.
It was a warm evening; lilac on the air.

Motels along the Turnpike
had lit up neon signs;
Welcome, they pulsed in scarlet.
Welcome. Welcome. Welcome.

DIDO IN HELL

I was in woods;
twilight, the green glow
of swamp-maple leaves, dank air,
then that figure,
unmistakable, moving out of shadow

towards me:
my almost wife;
a gaping wound at her breast, her face
white, staring, expressionless,
in her hand the hunting knife

I'd given her; blood-blackened now. A sound –
half sob, half hiss –
broke from my throat: it was true then.
What I'd heard was true: the measure taken.
Listen, I'm not responsible for this

I heard myself utter,
I never lied to you – my voice
rising, unsteady – *did I? did I?*
She stood in silence.
I had no choice! You knew I had no choice!

You knew . . . She'd gone though,
faded back into the woods.
Night fell. There were no stars;
only this tangling blackness
and my echoing words.

BLUES FOR SAMSON

My stylist
calls me darling,
says Hi I'm Dee, and asks what I'd like today, smiling.
My hair back, I tell her, my precious locks,
thick and unruly and glossy as they were
before I was fleeced.

Her laughter
as she switches
the clippers on, brings back that sweet-throated witch's
who comforted me as only your enemy can
in the days of my strength, when I smote
hip and thigh in a great slaughter.

Her nice eyes
by and by rest
on mine in the mirror. She leans in, letting her breast
brush against me. She knows her middle-aged man;
playing me like some trailer Delilah,
and I feel it rise;

the old blunt
want-instrument
that always and only wanted what it shouldn't;
Gaza, Timna, my Valley girl
who spilled me in broad daylight. I must have reckoned
the sun shone out of her cunt.

Too long now
bereft of it,
a woman's hands in my hair, or what's left of it,
is all I seem to require of love,
and all I'll spill is a tip, Dee; big as my straitened
circumstances allow,

for Dee, once
my head wasn't bare
as that cornfield after the foxes I set on fire
rampaged through it, or the orchards and olive groves
I flattened with my slat-armoured D9 'dozer,
but maned like a lion's.

GOLEM

I'm looking for the crack
where the yellowjackets nest.
I stumbled on it last summer
out here in the snakeroot
between the fence and the forest.
I had no idea
what it was that came boiling
out of that hidden fissure
in a sudden, upturned
blizzard of scalding gold,
only that its stings
were not the whiplash
of reflex, but some fury
my dead-weight must have roused
and in one long crackling flash
of white-hot letters
branded across my brow,
intent on rousing me: I ran,
flailing, incandescent,
in my own wheeling halo,
my suit of lightning, fire
racing through my astounded
body, my dumbstruck tongue
unscabbarding its word
up out of living bedrock
all that bright morning.

WATER SESSIONS I

– We had a fight. She threw her water at me.
My skin still feels hot
where it hit me: a splash-brand tingling

across my forehead – *What was the fight about?*
I don't remember. Nothing important.
The water's what I remember. It made me feel . . .

– *Yes?* – I want to say impotent
but that's not quite it; a stranger
debilitation as though I'd

absorbed some bone-melting toxin from her anger:
I can see the flung water still,
its chrome fingers probing towards me, elongating

like silvery staghorn coral,
and the splash, the impact, I can still feel that,
the soft catastrophic crash

like being spat at:
'Cracher'. . . I like the French word better;
juices your mouth and gives you the double disaster,

the spat-at but also the spitter,
like in *Nostromo*; that moment when Señor Hirsch,
hung from a beam by his elbows,

spits in his torturer's face, splash-crash,
– *You see yourself as her torturer?*
– No, but there does seem

some time-bending sorcery in the gesture;
a retro-fit, let's say, of the crime to the punishment,
backwardly flooding what one had thought quite harmless

with downright evil intent.
I mean, I had no more idea
of what I had coming, than the boy in the myth

Ceres spattered with wet grain for mocking her,
turning him into a scuttling lizard, as if
he could have known or imagined what it might mean

to step out, to walk his little life
into the ten-lane highway of a goddess's existence;
or Ascalaphus, splashed by Proserpine,

etched to a screech-owl in the instant's
acid-burn of underworld waters,
or Actaeon

who did nothing worse
than lose his way out hunting in a wood
and stumble on Diana skinny-dipping

when splash! The water antlered into his forehead
as she flung a scooped handful in rage,
as if being divine merely meant

being a flood in abeyance, an englobed deluge
primed for the instant engulfment
of anything too radically not itself,

at which the branching – *Excuse me, I think at this point*
you ought to tell me what the fight was about –
– at which the branching horns splashed out from his brow,

his ears furred over and sharpened, his hands and feet
hardened to hoofs, and off he stagger-galloped
chased by his own dogs

who sank their fangs in his hide and ripped
– *What was the fight about?*
– I told you, I don't remember, besides,

who ever really knows what a fight was about?
I mean you go in thinking it's one thing, then later
discover it was all along

some totally unrelated matter . . .

WOODPILE

The tolerant structure of a woodpile.
Two or more rows deep, each row end-stopped
by criss-crossing pairs of parallel logs
stacked up in columns: its one formal touch, and that optional,
otherwise a matter of simple accretion;
long or high as you want it; the piled chunks,
whether trapezoid in section, or half-moon, or witch-silhouette;
knobbed or bulbous, split like crocodile jaws,
or rock-hard uncrackable knots; whether
red oak, black cherry or yellow birch,
bearing each other's polyglot oddities
with an agglomerated strength, the opposite
of the engineer's soaring, cross-braced,
precision-cut glass and steel.

I make mine under a maple in the back yard,
from the five cords dumped there each year
by the cord-wood seller's dump-truck. Mindless work –
stooping, grabbing, chucking, stacking –
but I like it: the guaranteed satisfaction,
the exact ratio of effort to result;
how you can't fail at this if you put in the effort
any more than you can fake it if you don't,
and its endlessly forgiving form, that too; how a misplaced
or mischosen log doesn't matter,
how even when you think you're done
there's always room for another one on top;
everything coming out right in the end, more or less,
however clumsy its creator.

MR W.H.

Not that bloodlines,
family or otherwise
have ever meant much to me,
but at fifty one wants forebears
almost as much as heirs,
and even though the oblivion
we're headed for is doubtless
total, it feels somewhat
lonely heading there orphaned,
or lonelier than not.

Of course every poet
appoints his own ancestors
but that's one thing if you're Auden
enlisting Byron, another
if you're nobody claiming Auden.
Let me present, then,
(like one of those not quite kosher
relations in Jane Austen)
my mite of collateral evidence
connecting me with Wystan.

First, prep school; first cell in that hive
'whose honey is fear and worry' –
and not just any old holding pen
for the immature British toff,
but St Edmund's School, Hindhead, Surrey;
the school he and I both attended.
I doubt much had changed
in the fifty years between us,
from the stony puntabout
we waited on every third sunday

worried our distant parents
might forget or not bother to come,
to the horse-hair mattresses
we lay on, groping our way
to that potent formula
of pleasure, shame and repression
Freud had construed long before
as the jet-fuel of civilisation –
the energy-flight from Eros
to monuments, railways, war;

and that listless, indoor
golf-course of a landscape's
gravel drives and laurel hedges,
its buffed-to-a-gloss silver birches,
its insinuating mildness
that at best tamed us
into our bourgeois thrall to the 'ever so comfy',
not to mention our *penchant* for comfortable rhymes;
at worst so mimetically maimed us
as to make our – or anyway my –

utter loathing for it
a form of self-loathing . . .
Fast-forward twenty-five years
to my second exhibit:
a campus in New England –
old England on steroids;
the hills pumped up into mountains,
the little creosote potting sheds
swollen to ark-sized dairy barns anchored on meadows
big as counties.

I taught there in the nineties;
Auden in the forties.
Freshmen danced for him naked.
By my time the place
was a frontline in the battle
between the cerebral interest
and that of the, shall we say,
mailed fist?
Freedom – of thought, speech, dissent –
versus the President.

Freedom was losing badly:
tenure abolished, rumours
of impropriety spread,
eighteen professors fired;
the letter describing their protest
as *vengeful and selfish*;
you had to sign it
or risk being fired yourself.
Well, it wasn't Berlin or Spain
and doubtless wouldn't have merited

one line from Wystan's pen,
though the 'set mask of rectitude'
seems apropos – though again
the 'important Jew' who stripped it
has been all but stripped himself
from the approved shelf
by the professionally offended,
for putting (he might have put it)
the eros in generosity,
and though it isn't Vienna either

('Anna *bei Gestapo*')
there's a certain chill in the air;
Mastema, god of hatred, back in business,
working with equal zest
in the oppressor's uniform
and the rags of the oppressed;
you can track him by the bodies
dumped like a monster's faeces
in unexpected places;
while the last big thing that isn't yet ourselves,

out in the cold too long,
its face up against the glass,
window-crashes the party; and don't get me wrong:
I've seen those self-pitying monster-eyes
staring back out of mirrors;
I've felt the mounting
voluptuous hatred, the swell
of violence surge and foam from the littlest wound
to liquidate, if it could, conjectured
enemy-comrades, classes, whole nationalities,

and I accept my latent
guilt in the future
necessary murder
of my dearest neighbours; my hand,
if not yet dripping blood, at any rate ink-stained,
having said which, it's still Dame Kind –
unkillable *Tellus Mater* –
I choose to think of
as I look out over the barn porch
where the old hollow-hearted

crippled apple, all dad – what's the word?
daddock – all daddock and moss
and sagging, swirling-grained bulges,
stands like a fossilised
beggarwoman or sage:
dead, I'd thought, till I noticed
a cluster of green apples
like a branchful of underworld eyes
coolly regarding
my empty page.

THE EVENT

But did you imagine it would wait,
its fuse already lit, while you laboured
day and night for the exact word
to name what it was? Did you imagine it wouldn't
become without you what it hadn't with,
soonness always the point (you knew that though,
didn't you, didn't you? which is doubly tough).
Let go, ringed in its absence; crater or wreath:
all but posthumous now, your craving's token;
compliments to a former belle
not much noticed, whose heart lives in its aches
as in a peachstone the fire of peaches . . .
Things'll be fine, as far as you can tell,
but that show's over now, that wave has broken.

IT ISN'T ME

It isn't me, he'd say,
stepping out of a landscape
that offered, he'd thought, the backdrop
to a plausible existence
until he entered it; *it's just not me*,
he'd murmur, walking away.

It's not quite me, he'd explain,
apologetic but firm,
leaving some job they'd found him.
They found him others: he'd go,
smiling his smile, putting
his best foot forward, till again

he'd find himself reluctantly concluding
that this, too, wasn't him.
He wanted to get married, make a home,
unfold a life among his neighbours' lives,
branching and blossoming like a tree,
but when it came to it, *it isn't me*

was all he seemed to learn
from all his diligent forays outward.
And why it should be so hard
for someone not so different from themselves,
to find what they'd found, barely even seeking;
what gift he'd not been given, what forlorn

charm of his they'd had the luck to lack,
puzzled them – though not unduly:
they lived inside their lives so fully
they couldn't, in the end, believe in him,
except as some half-legendary figure
destined, or doomed, to carry on his back

24

the weight of their own all-but-weightless, stray
doubts and discomforts. Only sometimes,
alone in offices or living rooms,
they'd hear that phrase again: *it isn't me*,
and wonder, briefly, what they were, and where,
and feel the utter strangeness of being there.

WATCHER

In the lit space
between a fluorescent Chanel ad
and a cavern of duty-free Steuben,
herself less flesh and blood
than scent, it seems, and cut glass,
she settles in with her iPod
and a magazine.

He glances over;
feels it, that almost
outraged yearning, as if
for something he once possessed
and might yet recover
if he can just
make her turn for one brief

reciprocal look,
and he looks again, then again, each glance
a spray of sand
against an immense, glazed indifference
till at last, slowly, as if being tugged awake
out of its own separate trance,
her body stirs, and her hand

touches her things —
phone, laptop, coat —
and draws them in close
like some watchful spirit
armoured in bracelets and rings,
and that's all. It's not till she hears her flight
called in that air-brushing voice

fashioned, he half-imagines,
for summoning bored gods
and goddesses back to Olympus
on their own private clouds,
that she stands and deigns
to let the bright blue diodes
of her eyes rest on his

for a moment's glance,
then turns, the gesture
slow and deliberate,
as if to show him everything he'd ever
wanted but couldn't have; swans, stallions, dolphins
glittering as she takes it with her
calmly down the walkway to her gate.

A PEELED WAND

September clearness, insects
glinting on the far shore;
bullfrogs, red-wing blackbirds –
the dial-tone of summer –
bubbling up through the evening air . . .
Out on the water a snapper
snags a V of ripples
towards us – no, not a snapper . . .
We slow to a halt
as whatever it is circles closer
till we see him, suddenly clear in the water,
the curves of his half-submerged brow
bulging on the surface
like the smooth bulges on tree trunks
loggers call cat-face flaws;
forelegs working beneath him,
leisurely, as though walking on air;
and now, closer still,
in the bluestone-bottomed shallows,
he rises, holding aloft
the dripping boat of his head,
calmly scanning the bankside thickets,
then steps from the water,
lumbering right across our path,
and with two audible snips,
snips through an alder sapling
(the young bark still glossy brown)
in a salad of its own leaves
and shoulders it back to the shallows,
where, with the same unconcern,
he strips off and chews, one by one,
every twig and leaf,
washing each mouthful down
with a sip of our silver water

then glides off
for a between-courses swim
halfway across the reservoir,
paddle-tail wafting him
through a reflected mountain . . .
Winter now;
snow like wool, as the psalm says, mists like ashes.
I think of him out there again
in the late summer evening sweetness
of sumac and goldenrod,
swimming unhurriedly back
for the tender bark of the sapling;
turning the stick with his hands, nibbling
the tight skin clear from the greenwood —
all but a few tough inches at the thick end
left like a leather-bound hilt —
then with a last look around him
at the lilac-edged ring of mountains
and the sky like a jeweller's tray
with a sun and an opal moon
and two or three choice stars,
heading off back where he came from,
fanning a fishtail wake on the water
and leaving behind him the peeled wand
which I have here in my hand.

– But go back a moment
to that other dream,
about the river, remember,

the one half-hidden by trees, that time
you thought you'd dried up
– Yes, all cresses and willows

green-lit black water, swift and deep
– Narrow, you said
– Well, not the Hudson, an English river

– And you above it – Astride
more like, as if it flowed
from my own, you know, my loins

– Which felt? – Oh god, good!
– Like in that stranger's garden
in last night's dream?

– Go on . . .
– Your irrigation lines dry,
your own garden dead

– Which was most irrigating. Sorry.
– You followed the lines to the stream
which also turned out to be dry,

then climbed back upstream – Updream
– Way back, yes? To a fork
where all the water ran down the other fork

to the stranger's garden, which you say was like
– Paradise! The clear water brimming in fonts,
spilling over the beds, which stilled it

in ingots of gold squash, pepper plants;
held it in delicate scalloped or spear-tipped leaves,
musk melons heavy and scented like babies' heads,

tomatoes big as . . . big as boxing gloves;
I mean you could feel the surge of unimpeded
existence in every blissed-out sunburst corolla,

every collard leaf loaded
with waterglobes gleaming like gems on a shelf . . .
My god! – *Any idea who this stranger was?*

– None. – *You're sure?* – You want me to say myself
don't you? – *Do I?* – Some ghost-self perhaps,
one who'd either been spared whatever crime,

whatever irreparable lapse
from grace or luck that fork upstream represents
or else was himself the water thief,

as though I'd somehow stolen my own existence
from under my nose; somehow siphoned it off
elsewhere, like the Jordan waters

bled out into the roses of the Negev;
is that what you're saying? The dream
an effort, then, to reconcile certain polarities;

desert blossom, for instance, with suicide bomb,
or General Electric's 'We Bring Good Things to Light',
with the death-sludge they dumped in the Hudson,

or for that matter the British Mandate –
– *you're losing me* – Well, but it's true,
as heir to whatever misdeeds my own

triple axis – Anglo-American-Jew –
occasioned or outright did
before I became, as it were,

CEO of Myself Incorporated,
I might indeed wish to reconcile, even equate
certain opposites; villain and victim

tourist and terrorist; spitter even, and spat-at . . .
– *Which brings us back, does it not,*
to your fight. I think you should really –

– Like I said, who ever knows what a fight was about?
You go in thinking it's oil or land, and then later
discover it was all along only ever

about water . . .

LAST HARVEST

Abandoned houses have ghosts
to comfort them; each room
a cell of memory, rich in dusts
milled from the lives that furnished them.

No one lived in these homes,
and though they can't quite be called sad,
not being quite sentient (one assumes),
or knowing what they never had,

the way they stand there and wait,
unentered since their maker left
(too long ago to think they'll yet
be entered), makes them look bereft.

'Last harvest', farmers call it, but the cornfield
is greening back up through the cracked
black asphalt, while they fade unsold
above it, spoiling still intact,

and maybe just because they can't,
you yourself feel it all the more:
silence, stillness, and vacant
decades pressing at each door.

THE RUINED HOUSE

We passed these places
when we came this way before:
stone-towered fortress-farmhouses
going slowly to pieces
in a desolation of broom,
ilex and wild roses;
windows boarded, the spill
of terraces brambled over,
crumbling back into hill.

Someone explained it:
reform of the *mezzadrile*;
the old feudal peasantry
unbound from their vineyards,
their olive groves and beehives;
upgraded to wage-slaves.
No reason not to be elsewhere,
they left the land in droves,
went where the living was easier . . .

I had given up
a servitude of my own
to a no less exacting *padrone*;
Oh, I had broken
strong indentures, forsaken
the path of glory,
the discipline of the line,
for these paths of least resistance;
the sentence for the *sentiero*.

Now ten years later
I come full circle to find
the place in strange remission;
a posthumous *dolce vita*:
the houses newly young;
glazed, painted, repointed;
cisterns cleaned, doors rehung
a libidinous gleam
of Volvos under arbours.

So why do my spirits sink
and why do they rise again
at the one house all in ruins?
Why this gladness,
this unexpected relief
at the vine-spewing casements
and the front room's rank smash of rubble,
and the great, dank, black-fruited fig tree
erupting out of the roof?

BLUEBERRIES

I'm talking to you old man.
Listen to me as you step inside this garden
to fill a breakfast bowl with blueberries
ripened on the bushes I'm planting now,
twenty years back from where you're standing.
It's strictly a long-term project – first year
pull off the blossoms before they open,
second year let them flower, watch the bees
bobbing in every bonnet,
but don't touch the fruit till year three,
and then only sample a handful or two . . .
Old man I'm doing this for you!
You know what they say about blueberries:
blood-cleansing, mood-lifting memory-boosters;
every bush a little fountain of youth
sparkling with flavonoids, anthocyanin . . .
I've spent all summer clearing brush,
sawing locust poles for the frames,
digging in mounds of pine needles, bales of peat moss –
I thought I'd do it while I still could.
You can do something for me in turn:
think about the things an old man should;
things I've shied away from, last things.
Care about them only *don't* care too
(you'll know better than I do what I mean
or what I couldn't say, but meant).
Reconcile, forgive, repent,
but don't go soft on me; keep the faith,
our infidel's implicit vow:
'Not the hereafter but the here and now . . .'
Weigh your heart against the feather of truth
as the Egyptians did, and purge its sin,
but for your own sake, not your soul's.
And since the only certain

eternity's the one that stretches backward,
look for it here inside this garden:
Blueray, Bluecrop, Bluetta, Hardy Blue;
little fat droplets of transsubstantiate sky,
each in its yeast-misted wineskin, chilled in dew.
This was your labour, these are the fruits thereof.
Fill up your bowl old man and bring them in.

DUST

We were children here,
biblical siblings,
mauling each other on the cave-floor
of the workshop and the playroom.

Adults now,
together on housework detail:
we roll up the old white living-room rug,
lug it out on our shoulders

like the hide of some ancient beast
we'd tracked down in its lair,
slinging it up between the fence and the tool-shed,
and laying into it, each with a thick iron bar,

you on one side, me on the other,
slamming it hard, with a thud
and a burst of dust at each blow, the dust
chalking the air till our eyes

smart, and we're choking and have to stop for it to clear,
then stand there watching it
floating like some glinting amorphous ghost,
down the garden and over the fields below.

ANCHISES

after Virgil

Your ghost, father,
always before me,
led me down to this place;
my ships are tugging at their anchors,
but give me
give me your hand
let me embrace you
don't draw back, father . . .
Tears brimmed in his eyes, spilled over;
three times he threw his arms round his father's neck
three times the shade slipped through
into thin air like a dream.

BITTERSWEET

In your book, success
was a dirty word, wealth
even dirtier, fame
not to be uttered;
the work was all that mattered.
I took that to heart I guess,
in my own monkish fashion:
'So much to say no to
before you can start to say yes'
having long been my motto.
No, for instance,
to the bittersweet
I'm trying to extirpate
from under the garden fence.
I'd thought nothing of it
except that its berries
might brighten the wires in fall
like a coat of arms on a wall,
but it's taken over the place:
lost, one has to assume,
in the delirium
of its own joyous work
of making the universe
or at any rate this fence
a monument, shall we say,
to its own magnificence;
and not just this mass of scarlet, orange-winged berries
seething like a swarm of underworld bees,
or the intractable tanglings
of vines like stiffened springs,
but these astounding roots also:
blood-bright, trailing their corpse-hair capillaries
down through the topsoil. I yank them out

only to find they've coiled right down through the shale
into solid bedrock,
leaving a lizard tail in each crack
potent enough to grow the whole lizard back
just in case there remained any doubt, any question
as to the error, the sheer utter folly of planning
a garden of one's own
where bittersweet has grown.

INDUSTRY BAY

Here's your grandson clowning in the ocean;
scuttling out of the waves then bossing them back.
He looks more like you every minute;
beetling his brow in the same mock frown you made.
Here's a hammock without you lying in it;
a sea-grape tree without you in its shade.
And here's me, taking the measure of your absence;
failing again; stalled like that restless palm top
flapping its chicken feathers in the sun
while overhead some wide-winged ocean bird
rises on the breezes without effort
as if to tell me: *this is how it's done . . .*

THING ONE AND THING TWO

The gelding knife
they showed me on the farm
was an adjustable, steel-tendoned instrument,
part plier, part caliper,
with two raw-edged sickle moons
that opened on springs and closed
like crab claws: the deed, it appeared,
requiring as complex a harm
as the harm it opposed.

The box of hardcore porn
I found in the woods
was softened by rain,
its pinks and purples leached to bluey greys,
bloated flesh splitting open
under my fumbling, impatient touch,
with a reeking sweetness.
I was queasy with it for days.
Then I went there again.

The billy goat
was up on his hind legs, in rut;
blethering, poking his tongue out, frotting the fence,
slit-pupilled yellow eyes rolling, coat
glistening gold like an archbishop's cloak
from his damascene drip and drool.
The farmer cocked his adamantine tool.
'Snip snip and Bob's your auntie,'
as my father used to joke.

My son
sprawls in my lap, naked,
frolicking with his own
delinquent cat in a hat
while things one and two run amok
in his bedtime book,
and all this comes back
as an urge – I suppress it –
to stop him.

LULLABY

Little tortoise, stretching
your thumb's length of neck
from the crib of my son's hand
with the ready-to-go look
of a toy fresh from its box,
you haven't grasped yet, have you,
what it is to be you –

that what you are, even now
happened too long ago
for any extent of newness
or eagerness, to undo;
that the Adam of your species
asked for what he asked for,
and the gods granted his wishes?

Settle down then, tuck
your head in its leather sock;
you don't need anything
and nothing's required of you;
only to turn,
slowly and without pain
into your own stone urn

while the world reels by
unintelligibly,
faster as you grow slower;
spring and fall flashing round
like fairground horses, a flower
there and gone like a firework,
your child grown old in an hour.

THE MEN QUESTION TIRESIAS

But tell us, did things look
different, not having a cock –
trees, for instance, or water,
or a juicy steak?

Did mirrors grow sticky
when you tried to pass by?
Is it true what they showed you was more like fiction
than autobiography?

And would those kinds of
questions have turned you right off
the kind of man who could ask them?
And what about love –

did it lose its
air of being in quotes?
Was it as simple and real as bread?
As necessary as boots?

Was what you wanted
something we actually had?
Or were we just better than nothing?
Not even as good?

And lastly, if being in the sack
female's the better fuck,
then why, if you don't mind us asking,
did you switch back?

DOG DAYS

Blizzard died. I'm remembering
his limitless affection;
how he constantly gave you the chance to open your heart,
to thaw some of the ice around it;
how I failed to respond; knowing I should, but unable,
as if some crucial defeat would thereby be registered,
though even as I complained about him tramping mud all over
   the house,
or filling the snow in the yard with piss stains and frozen turds
or getting his muzzle full of porcupine quills,
or jumping bang through the screen door, or licking the butter,
or costing a fortune in pills and shots;
how, behind my posture of annoyance, behind my frosty hostility,
I knew him to be a princely spirit, magnanimous;
knew it from how he greeted me after every rebuff
with his jumps and nuzzles;
every day saying 'this is your chance to show love . . .'
Why couldn't I show it?
Why this sense that good as it might have been,
it would also have been a violation of the natural order
or my own personal order?
I see him,
trotting ahead in the woods,
the big white plume of his tail bobbing up and up
like an irrepressible fountain, then vanishing
as he thundered off after a squirrel.
When he slept, his flank would start quivering;
he'd draw back his ears and his muzzle, and moan with delight,
chasing the squirrel again in his dreams.
Once, while I lay on the couch, flattened by depression,
he came and placed his paw in my hand,
and made a pitiful, pitying baying sound.

I did feed and water him, even cleaned up his shit once in a while,
but always with a dutiful air, an aggrieved look of martyrdom
as though afraid our household would collapse
if someone in it didn't preserve a certain stiffness,
a certain chilliness in regard to the purely creaturely.

MAILBOXES, ELECTION DAY 2008

You see them at corners
of driveways and rural roads:
lines of metal mailboxes
set neatly on a single beam,
each with its own diagonal brace, jutting forward;
uniform, unassuming, unremarkable,
unless their knees-up angles
happen to make you think of soldiers
frozen in goose-stepping motion,
which they wouldn't unless you'd seen by contrast
that rickety assemblage – or something like it –
of a dozen-odd different-shaped canisters
on a frame of warped, silvered wood
I drove by last summer
on a back road in the old Gilboa Forest;
some of them painted with stars, some covered
with trumpet vines, some in a swarm
of orange geraniums, or dangled over
by butterfly shoals of oxalis, the whole dented,
drunkenly tilting row like some battered chorus-line
doing the can-can, each to its own different drummer, though why,
of all things, these should come back
at this of all moments,
I couldn't exactly say: it's as if
the tidings they'd all along, without knowing,
been decked out like that to receive
were coming in suddenly, wave after wave,
bringing the whole crazed contraption
back into flower, and I'm feeling
like one of those dumbstruck sailors
caught in the salt-blue crystal of myth
as they realise what they have on board,
green vines bursting from their decks and mast
ivy spurting out of their oars.

You made up? – We just let it go.
It seemed suddenly possible:
a change of mood like a change of season;

nothing in our control
other than being ours to accept or not
– *And you did?* – We went for a walk

up to the lookout.
Below us already vivid
powdery bud-sprays rolled like smoke through the
    valley.

I hadn't realised spring had arrived.
Under the ridge-snow a sheet
of meltwater slid over grasses and mosses,

new ferns scoping up through the rubble of slate . . .
That other kingdom, going about its business,
there for you if you want it, waiting

like a long-suffering friend, or former mistress;
post-diluvian, sexless, second best,
knowing your weaknesses, forgiving them . . .

– *And so?* – It started raining. We kissed
in the damp shelter of a cliff,
dodging crashing icicles. Luminous

ice-glazed birches dripped and wept. Far off,
curving over the Hudson,
the bridge lay glittering like a ring.

And that none of this, not the rain,
nor this unexpected reprieve,
would go on forever seemed strangely . . .

– *Yes?* – Fair, I guess. Fair enough.

TO A PESSIMIST

It's true: the chances
that good luck won't stop dropping in your lap
are, as they are of most things, mostly against;
that whether looked at from this or the far side of fences,
the grass is basically ashes,
and that half-full or -empty, the best-laid glass
invariably smashes.

But before you bury
your head in a dune of Zoloft,
remember – speaking of odds – the sheer oddness
of being brought into this sunlit, sublunary
existence's bosom
out of the black, like some ancient ironwood's
improbable blossom.

To be born, to have hollowed
this singular passage, the exact
outline of yourself, through the rock of ages,
argues, does it not, that one might be allowed
if not to aspire
to outright happiness, then at least to resist
abject despair?

Your house will fall down, for sure,
followed – who knows? – by the sky itself,
but not today, and probably not tomorrow,
and bear in mind also, that despite the law
that returns must diminish,
the gods, when they act at all, have been known to bless
as well as to punish.

STONES

I'm trying to solve the problem of the paths
between the beds. A six-inch cover
of cedar chips that took a month to lay
rotted in two years and turned to weeds.
I scraped them up and carted them away,
then planted half a sack of clover seeds
for a 'living mulch'. I liked that: flowers
strewn along like stars, the cupid's bow
drawn on each leaf like thumbnail quartermoons,
its easy, springy give – until it spread
under the split trunks framing off each bed,
scribbling them over in its own
green graffiti . . . I ripped it out
and now I'm trying to set these paths in stone.
It isn't hard to find: the ground here's littered
with rough-cut slabs, some of them so vast
you'd think a race of giants must have lived here
building some bluestone Carnac or Stonehenge,
us their dwindled offspring, foraging
among their ruins . . . I scavenge
lesser pieces; pry them from the clutches
of tree-roots, lift them out of ditches,
filch them from our own stone wall
guiltily, though they're mine to take,
then wrestle them on board the two-wheeled dolly
and drag them up the driveway to the fence,
where, in a precarious waltz, I tip
and twist them backward, tilting all their weight
first on one corner, then the other
and dance them slowly through the garden gate.
The hard part's next, piecing them together;
a matter of blind luck and infinite pains:
one eye open for the god-given fit –
this stone's jagged key to that one's lock –

the other quietly gauging how to fudge it:
split the difference on angles, cram the gaps
with stone-dust filler; hoping what the rains
don't wash away, the frost will pack and harden . . .
A chipmunk blinks and watches from his rock,
wondering if I've lost my mind perhaps.
Perhaps I have; out here every day,
cultivating – no, not even that;
tending the inverse spaces of my garden
(it's like a blueprint now, for Bluebeard's castle),
while outside, by degrees, the planet slips
– a locking piece – into apocalypse,
but somehow I can't tear myself away:
I like the drudgery; I seem to revel
in pitting myself against the sheer
recalcitrance of the stones; using
their awkwardness – each cupped or bulging face,
every cockeyed bevel and crooked curve,
each quirk of outline (this one a cracked lyre,
that one more like a severed head) –
to send a flickering pulse along the border
so that it seems to ripple round each bed
with an unstonelike, liquid grace:
'the best stones in the best possible order'
or some such half-remembered rule in mind,
as if it mattered, making some old stones
say or be anything but stone, stone, stone;
as if these paths might serve some purpose
aside from making nothing happen; as if
their lapidary line might lead me somewhere –
inward, onward, upward, anywhere
other than merely back where I began,
wondering where I've been, and what I've done.